How to Budget for Young Adults
A Practical Guide

© Copyright 2022 - All rights reserved.

The content contained within this book may not be reproduced, duplicated, or transmitted without direct written permission from the author or the publisher.

Under no circumstances will any blame or legal responsibility be held against the publisher, or author, for any damages, reparation, or monetary loss due to the information contained within this book, either directly or indirectly.

Legal Notice:

This book is copyright protected. It is only for personal use. You cannot amend, distribute, sell, use, quote or paraphrase any part, or the content within this book, without the consent of the author or publisher.

Disclaimer Notice:

Please note the information contained within this document is for educational and entertainment purposes only. All effort has been executed to present accurate, up to date, reliable, complete information. No warranties of any kind are declared or implied. Readers acknowledge that the author is not engaging in the rendering of legal, financial, medical, or professional advice. The content within this book has been derived from various sources. Please consult a licensed professional before attempting any techniques outlined in this book.

By reading this document, the reader agrees that under no circumstances is the author responsible for any losses, direct or indirect, that are incurred as a result of the use of information contained within this document, including, but not limited to, errors, omissions, or inaccuracies.

Table of Contents

Introduction

Chapter 1: The Basics of Budgeting

How Do You Start Budgeting?

Chapter 2: Creating Good Spending Habits

Identifying Spending Triggers

Track Your Spending

Ditch the Credit Card

Have Short-Term Goals

Better Pricing Options

Chapter 3: Implementing Saving Habits

Savings and Emergency Budgets

Celebrate the Milestones

Make Use of Automatic Transfers

Setting Savings Goals

Chapter 4: Coming Up with Financial Life Goals

Setting Financial Goals

Achieving Financial Goals

Chapter 5: Practicing Financial Discipline

What Is Financial Self-Discipline?

How to Deal with Financial Issues

Why Do Financial Problems Arise?

Why Is It Challenging to Be Financially Disciplined?

How to Be Self-Disciplined with Money

Chapter 6: Building a Healthy Relationship with Money

Signs You Have an Unhealthy Relationship with Money

Why Do We Develop Unhealthy Relationships with Money?

How to Build a Healthy Relationship with Money

Conclusion

References

Introduction

Do you want to learn how to manage your finances to secure your future?

If your answer is yes, you've come to the right place.

This book will teach you about budgeting and managing your finances so that you can start off on the right foot!

You must have heard the following statement when people talk about finances, "It's never too early to start," and "Time is your best friend." While you might know how important it is to budget and save money properly, most young people are unsure where to start. Also, most think that if they start budgeting, they will have to deprive themselves of everything. That is as far away from what budgeting actually is as possible. In reality, it means knowing where every penny you have is and knowing how much you spend on what and how to plan accordingly.

Budgeting can help you make smarter financial decisions. Not only can this help you save money, but it can also keep you prepared for any emergency. Learning how to keep track of your finances can help you get out of debt and focus on bigger goals.

Budgeting is not just a skill but a lifelong habit we all need to practice. This book will teach you how to regularly and easily plan your budget.

Chapter 1: The Basics of Budgeting

So, you've finally attained financial independence and can now spend money on the things you want. But since you are reading this, you understand that this freedom comes with serious responsibilities and questions such as:

- Am I spending too much money?
- Is my rent too much?
- What amount should I be saving each month, and how should I save?
- Should I feel guilty every time I go on a shopping spree?

Well, the answers to all these questions come down to budgeting your money. When you budget, you will understand if your rent is too high and if you can afford to go out every weekend.

But budgeting isn't just crucial for understanding your spending. Here are a few more reasons you should be budgeting your money:

It Prepares You for Future 'Adulting'

If you've never heard this before, here's the thing about adulting - The older you get, the more expenses you'll have to think about. Things like buying a home, paying bills, kids' expenses, etc.

As a young adult, you probably don't have a lot on your plate right now, so if you learn good money habits now, it will be easier when you are older. Besides, you will have a smaller financial burden when things get tough as you can tap into your accumulated savings and investments.

You Can Afford Your Desired Lifestyle

You probably want to do a lot before life gets 'serious,' and truth be told, this is the best time to do all those things as you are still free from major responsibilities.

When you budget well, you will be surprised at how many things you can squeeze out of your income. You would be able to get rid of unnecessary expenses and focus on what you truly want.

No More Panicking!

Life is uncertain, and you always fear and stress about the unknown when you don't have a cushion for unexpected expenses. You never know when car problems may arise or if you will accidentally chip a tooth and require a visit to the dentist, and so on.

But when you budget your money and set aside a few dollars here and there, even when emergencies come up, you know you can take care of them.

How Do You Start Budgeting?

You will need to work out three things before you start budgeting your money. These are:

1. Your income
2. Your expenses

3. Your desired savings, investments, and unplanned expenses

Let's look into each one in more detail.

You might want to get a notebook and a pen. Be ready to do some quick math.

1. Income

When it comes to your income, you will need to include every source. The point of budgeting is to make sure that every penny goes to something specific. If you don't, you may be tempted to spend money haphazardly.

You need to remember that your income is so much more than just your paycheck. Think about any monetary gifts you've received, side hustles, online rewards, cashback on your purchases, tax returns, and bank interest.

Keep track of all these sources of income separately, especially since they may not be reliable or generate a fixed amount of money each month. You can allocate a folder or file for these extra income sources.

Here are a few questions you can ask yourself to determine all your sources of income:

How much is my income (after tax)?

How many sources of income do I have, and how much do I make from each one?

Do I receive financial aid from anyone? How much and how often do I get this aid?

If you have a business, approximately how much profit do you make from it every month?

Make sure to include every income stream.

Once you have that sorted, you need to start using an income tracker.

You can use a notebook to record your monthly income amounts if you're not tech-savvy. After calculating your total, you need to eliminate expenses, determine how much you will save, and, if you want, find out how much money you plan to give out to charity.

If you can handle technology, an Excel spreadsheet can be a great way to keep track of all those things. You can create a column for your income sources, one for each month of the year, and a row at the very bottom for the total. It would be wise to split each column for every month into two additional columns: gross and net.

2. Expenses

Keeping track of your expenses can give you a better insight into where your money is going. This step is crucial if you want to develop better spending habits and save more money.

Checking all your account statements, including your credit cards, and checking accounts, can help you pinpoint where you're spending your money. Next, start grouping your expenses. This will be a reality check if you're an impulse buyer.

Creating another spreadsheet for your fixed and variable expenses is also important. It will help you to get better clarity about your situation. Your fixed expenses are probably going to stay the same each month. This is why variable expenses are easier to control unless you have monthly subscriptions you can do without. Having everything laid out before you makes it easier to see if there's room for change.

3. Savings, Investments, and Unplanned Expenses

Now that you've eliminated your unnecessary expenses, you need to consider what you want in terms of savings and investments and your unplanned expenses. According to the amount of money you have left, work out how much money you want to save or invest. This is vital if you have future plans or goals that you want to achieve. Whether you want to buy a house, a car, or travel the world, you need to start saving as early as possible. Make sure to account for any unexpected or emergency expenses and set extra money aside.

When you're budgeting your income, there are several aspects to account for. Staying organized and keeping track of everything that comes in and goes out of your bank account is key.

Chapter 2: Creating Good Spending Habits

Many of us start the month with the best intentions possible, to spend our money wisely. However, before we know it, window shopping turns into "it's on sale… I'll never be able to get it for that price again," and one night out with your friends turns into a weekly get-together. We can beat ourselves up and cry over spilled milk. Everyone knows that this is never a solution.

One of two ways to go from there is to either find comfort in the fact that you're not the only one with this issue or set out to make a change. You may be overspending for many reasons, and guesstimating your income and expenses may be one of them. Fortunately, following the advice from Chapter 1 can help with that. In this chapter, you will find out how you can create good spending habits to help with your overspending problem.

Identifying Spending Triggers

We all have our weak spots when it comes to spending our money. Fashion enthusiasts, for instance, can't hold their purses closed when it comes to clothes. Artists may spend all their money on paintbrushes. Equestrians are known for their obsession with saddle pads, and tech enthusiasts may struggle to curb their spending when new devices hit the market. What is your weak shopping spot?

You need to determine your triggers to keep your spending under control. Think about your hobbies and interests and avoid these temptations, thus removing the opportunity to spend great amounts of money.

Think about whether you tend to have more energy during certain times of the day. Do your energy levels influence your shopping or spending habits? Do you spend more money when you're energetic, or does it help you make better spending choices? When you're low on energy, are you too tired to shop, or do you buy everything that seems mildly appealing?

You should also think about the surrounding environment. We all find ourselves in certain places where we simply have no control over our spending or feel pressured to spend while we're there. Naturally, you'll find it hard to maintain control if you visit all your favorite stores. Some places, such as festivals, shopping malls, bazaars, and funfairs, also pressure you to spend a lot of money.

Our mood is another thing that influences our buying patterns. Some people indulge in retail therapy when they're feeling under the weather. Others may go on impulsive shopping sprees when excited, believing everything to be a great deal.

We also spend more money when we're out with our friends. Going out with friends, especially those who struggle with managing their finances, can cause us to spend more money than we usually do. If your friends like to shop and dine at very expensive places, you don't have to go out with them on those occasions. You could also suggest less expensive plans to your friends. You can chat over coffee instead of meeting up for drinks, explore nature instead of going to music festivals, or have cozy movie nights at home instead of going to the movies.

Your parents' lifestyle may also affect your financial decisions. If you were used to living on a tight budget before being financially independent, you might feel compelled to spend money on everything you want. If you were living comfortably, you might also try to keep up with that lifestyle, which can put a lot of financial strain on you.

Track Your Spending

As mentioned in the previous chapter, you must keep track of your spending to create good spending habits. You shouldn't just record your fixed expenses, such as rent and monthly internet, streaming services, gym subscriptions, etc. The best way to track your spending is to record all your purchases, no matter how small. If you visit the supermarket, keep the receipt in a folder. If you buy a pencil at the stationery shop, make sure to write it down. You need to be aware of where your money is going because once you reflect on your spending habits, you'll be able to make better financial decisions. If you save as little as $5 a day, that will add up to $150 a month.

Ditch the Credit Card

Credit cards are both a blessing and a curse. Nothing seems easier than pulling out your credit card and paying with it. It saves you the embarrassment of trying to fit all the change into your wallet while the person next to you in the queue waits their turn. Unfortunately, credit cards are one of the biggest reasons for overspending.

While your credit card gives you the temporary relief of not seeing your physical bills increase with every purchase, you may be surprised that you have spent more than you can afford by the end of the month. After identifying your monthly spending budget, allocate a specific amount of money to spend each week. If you find yourself running low on cash, you'll have to figure out how to make it work.

If you need to go to the grocery store, only take the amount of money you think you'd need and leave your credit card at home. This will stop you from making impulse purchases. Having your credit card information saved on all your favorite online stores can also cause you to make many unnecessary purchases. If you delete the saved information and enter it every time you purchase, you'll have more time to think about whether you really need the item or not.

Have Short-Term Goals

Aside from the big goals, such as saving enough money to buy your dream home, having attainable short-term goals can help keep you motivated. Your goals shouldn't be generic, such as "decreasing the amount of money I spend on coffee." Make sure to mention numbers and a timeframe. A more effective goal would be "cutting down my spending on coffee from $140 a month to $70 a month." When you start small and with a specific target in mind, you will soon apply the same strategy to other aspects of your spending. This will get you into the habit of being more economic in life. Instead of eating out at work or university every day, you'll soon make it a habit to pack your own lunch.

Better Pricing Options

You also need to start taking advantage of special offers and deals. However, this doesn't mean you should spend money on things you don't need just because of a discount. For instance, if you want to buy a new phone, but you know that its price will be reduced two months from now, it's not going to hurt to wait a little longer. If you want to buy a car, you can look around for used cars that are still in good condition. You don't need a brand new one if you can't afford it at the moment. You can also compare the prices at different stores or vendors whenever there's anything you want to buy.

Knowing your spending triggers, keeping track of your expenses, minimizing your credit card usage, acquiring short-term goals, and exploring better pricing options can help you create good spending habits. However, these changes will not be enough if you aren't properly budgeting your monthly income.

Chapter 3: Implementing Saving Habits

Saving money is one of the hardest things to do in life. As long as we know we have the money, even when we really want to save it, it can be very hard not to spend it on the things we want. We all have our temptations, and it only gets harder to curb them when we know we can afford them.

Having leftover money after covering all your essentials may persuade you to buy less important stuff. To be fair, life gets in the way most of the time. We sometimes try to avoid all spending triggers and steer clear of window shopping just for the washing machine to break down. Soon, before you know it, you're back to square one on your savings efforts. However, after reading this chapter, you will find out how to create and implement effective saving habits.

Savings and Emergency Budgets

As you know by now, budgeting is the most important thing for managing your finances. We mentioned in chapter 1 that you need to allocate a monthly budget for your savings and another for emergency expenses. Make sure to meet both budgets, no matter what, each month, even if it means that you'll have to sit out some outings or pack your own lunches. By having an emergency budget, you'll be able to avoid taking some money out of your savings envelope when things get rough.

Celebrate the Milestones

We tend to be very harsh with ourselves, especially when it comes to financial matters. If we save $5, we will keep wondering why we didn't save $10. If we make it to $100, we criticize ourselves for not saving $150. However, we need to remember that saving money is not an easy task and that every penny saved does matter.

It doesn't matter if you ended up saving $5 or $100, because what truly matters is that you did set something aside. You need to start somewhere, and the best way to go about saving money, like everything else in the world, is to start slowly and gradually. You can't dive right in and decide to save 40% of your monthly income. This will never work if you are used to using up all your money. You need time to adjust to your new lifestyle, experiment, and decide what things you can live without.

Allow yourself to start slow and pick up the pace as you go. Remind yourself that there's nothing to worry about as long as you're headed in the right direction. If you end up saving only $30 a month, that's $360 a year! Besides, you're not only doing this for the money. You're doing it to establish a lifelong habit: It not only helps you achieve financial independence, but it also teaches you invaluable skills, such as dedication, determination, goal-setting, responsibility, planning, and adaptability.

Make Use of Automatic Transfers

You can save money without giving it much thought if you set up automatic transfers to your savings account from your checking account. Before doing that, you must have a fixed budget for your savings. You must also have consistent, attainable, and realistic goals for your savings and expenses.

If you're not using the same bank for your savings and checking accounts, consider doing so, as it will make the process much easier. All you'd need to do is set up a savings account for each goal you have. Then, start the monthly automatic transfers between both accounts.

If you're using the same bank for both accounts, you may also be able to have your direct deposit divided. This way, the bulk of your paycheck will go into your checking account, while your decided percentage or dollar amount will go into your savings account. This can make the saving process much easier and painless because the money will go straight into your savings account as if it weren't there, to begin with.

Setting Savings Goals

As we mentioned before, to save money, you need to have goals. Otherwise, you won't have any motivation to save and will probably give up after a couple of months. Think about what you're saving for. These could be both long-term and short-term goals. Do you want to get married? Do you want to go on your dream vacation to Paris? Are you dying for that brand new Fendi purse? Perhaps you want to retire at 45 years old. No matter your goals, you need to find out the exact amount of money you need and set up a realistic timeframe for the amount of time it will take you to save it.

Goals that can be achieved in the near future are typically set within a one to three-year timeframe. This could include having an emergency fund covering all your living expenses for six months, having enough money to go on a well-deserved vacation, or saving up money to afford a down payment for a new car. It could be all of these goals, too. It all depends on your income, budget, will, and desire.

Future-oriented goals are any goals set beyond the next three years. These could be purchasing a new home, saving enough money to cover your child's tuition, or preparing for retirement. The goals you set depend on your priorities and your lifestyle. You can set as many goals as you want, as long as they're reasonable and achievable. Remember that one person's idea of what's reasonable differs from another's. It all depends on your current income and financial situation.

If you're saving for something huge, like your retirement plan or child's tuition, putting your money in a 529 plan, an IRA or any other investment account can be a great idea. Although investments are risky, they offer a great opportunity for financial growth. They are especially beneficial for anything you plan for early on (your long-term goals).

Rewards

Don't skimp on small, short-term goals. These can serve as fun rewards for your efforts. Try to keep these goals big enough so that you will not always have the needed cash to pay for them, but not large enough to leave you in debt or compromise your long-term goals. This can be a new smartphone, small gifts for your birthday or the holidays, or even a full spa treatment. Smaller goals and fun rewards are psychologically proven to pay off. Seeing immediate or visible results can help you reinforce the habit of saving.

Priorities

Focusing on long-term or big targets can be tempting when setting your goals. For instance, you may be compelled to save up for a huge country retirement home with a large barn or set out to retire in Italy. Obviously, the more financially demanding your long-term goals are, the more compromises you're going to have to make regarding your short-term needs. You need to allocate your savings mindfully and set realistic goals. If your long-term goals cause you to become stingy with your money or fall short of your current needs, then you may need to rethink your priorities.

Saving money is much easier said than done. Because so many people struggle to set money aside, you're doing your future self a huge favor by establishing this habit early on in life.

Chapter 4: Coming Up with Financial Life Goals

Setting financial life goals is one of the most fundamental aspects of budgeting. You will not be able to keep up your saving if you don't have a good reason to do it. You need goals to push you forward and motivate you.

Goals are the foundation of plans. You can't make plans if you don't know your final destination. Everyone knows that maneuvering through life without a solid outline is a recipe for failure. You need to look ahead and get a clear view of the big picture. You need to know what you want to do with your money and devise a schedule or plan to get there. After you've come up with your goals, this is when you can finally put your good financial habits into practice.

By reading this chapter, you will learn how to set and achieve your financial goals.

Setting Financial Goals

We've discussed the importance of setting savings goals throughout the previous chapter. We also provided some insight into how you can do it. However, we didn't go into full detail about how you can set sustainable goals and achieve them. Goals should be set for every aspect of your finances, not just your savings.

You can set your financial goals in just six steps:

1. Introspection

You will have to do a bit of soul-searching in this first step. You need to figure out everything that matters to you and all you want to achieve in life. Think about how you see yourself in the future.

Do you want to give back to your parents?

Do you see yourself as an employee or a boss? If you want to run the show, do you plan on opening your own business?

Do you want to/currently have kids? If so, what are their current/future needs?

Think about everything you want and care about, regardless of how far off they may be. Think about tomorrow, next month, and the next ten years. This is your chance to put everything on the table.

2. Weigh It Out

Now that you know what you want and have laid everything out as an option, you need to weigh it up. What is within reach and what seems rather whimsical? A trip around Europe is manageable. However, owning a castle may not be too realistic.

Think about your current income and whether you expect it to grow/decrease within the next few years. Remember your current definition of "possible" may change in 10 years. Maybe by then, owning a castle would actually be possible. Regardless, keep in mind that you must be realistic while setting your goals.

3. SMART Goals

When setting goals, you need to think SMART. SMART goals are always Specific, Measurable, Attainable, Relevant, and Timely.

Let's say you need a new car (relevant goal) and believe you can afford a Mercedes in five years; you shouldn't just write down "buy a car." Instead, an example of a SMART goal would be:

"I am going to buy the newest model, C180 Mercedes, in exactly five years." This is more specific, measurable (you can measure whether you can buy a Mercedes or another cheaper car), and timely.

4. Realistic Budget

After setting your goals, you need to determine the budget you need to achieve each of these goals and set a rough timeframe. What can be achieved in the near future, and what needs a bit more time? The budget you allocate to each of these goals should depend on your income and fixed expenses.

Consider the amount of money you plan to invest and the portion of your savings you want to use for each goal. When setting your goals, you need to keep every aspect of your finances in mind. As we mentioned before, you shouldn't compromise your current needs to fulfill lofty goals.

5. Separate Account

The chances are that your tight budget and the possible overestimation of expenses will leave you with a few extra dollars. If this doesn't happen, you shouldn't worry. Supposedly, you have a good amount of money set aside for emergencies. If you have leftover cash, you should distribute it among your topmost priorities.

6. Keep Track

As you know, great goals are always measurable. This is why you must track your progress and ensure you hit mentionable milestones. If you think you're slacking, it's time to go back and figure out what went wrong.

Achieving Financial Goals

When you set your goals, you may feel at a loss about how you should approach them. This is why prioritizing them becomes crucial. While setting your budget, you may have realized that some goals could be achieved earlier than others. To keep an organized timeline, it's a good idea to draw up a goal chart for each of your goals.

Developing a Goal Chart

1. Write down your SMART goal
2. Find out whether it's a **short-term**, a **mid-term**, or a **long-term** financial goal.

Short-term financial goals are the goals that you can achieve in under one year. Since these goals are within a limited time scope, you'll have more clarity about the general circumstances. If you are serious about these goals, you will have to get a grip on your spending habits, diminish debt, and start saving and funding for emergencies.

Home improvements, paying off debt, and finishing your degree are examples of short-term goals.

Mid-term financial goals don't take many years to achieve yet can't be reached in just a few months. The goals can take you two to five years to achieve, and they can usually be pulled off by having multiple income streams.

Starting a business, paying off student loans, and putting a down payment on a house can all be considered mid-term goals.

Long-term financial goals are goals that will take you five or more years to accomplish. These goals are the big ones - the expensive ones, and require a lot of time, patience, and dedication.

Your retirement plan, paying off your mortgage, and paying for your children's college tuition (no debt involved) are all examples of long-term goals.

3. Determine the exact amount of money you need to achieve that goal. Then break it down into a monthly or yearly amount.

4. Figure out which measures you need to take to achieve that goal.

Do you need to cut your expenses? Will you work overtime? Will you find another source of income?

5. You'll probably have to take more than one measure. Write them down and get started.

If you're tackling several goals at once, keep in mind that you'll have to coordinate your budget allocation. Don't rush your timeline; one person's short-term goal can be another's long-term one. If you can buy a house in three years but have other short-term and mid-term goals to cover, gathering the down payment can take you longer than anticipated.

Goal-setting is a very important part of managing your finances. It can seem very overwhelming at first. However, once you find out what you want and ensure that all your goals are specific, measurable, attainable, relevant, and timely, you will be able to approach them effectively.

Chapter 5: Practicing Financial Discipline

Three main factors to maintaining financial stability are self-discipline, self-control, and self-mastery. Lacking those three important characteristics, regardless of your income, can cause you to fall into a spiral of financial problems. Money and wealth are very volatile. Life itself is also very unpredictable. You can struggle to pay rent one day and find yourself climbing the corporate ladder the next. The opposite is also true. This is why you should never assume that things will stay as they are, especially when dealing with money.

There are thousands of stories and live examples of people who were incredibly wealthy one day and ended up on the streets the next -after their business took a dive or were let go from their positions at work. Taking a look at their net worth, you would expect that they would've been able to sustain a reasonable standard of living until they've had the chance to figure things out. However, their lack of self-discipline is what led to their downfall.

We struggle with self-discipline and control when we're unable to delay our need for short-term gratification. The more we struggle with this problem, the more likely we are to spend every penny we earn. We may even go beyond our incomes and start getting into debt ourselves by resorting to using credit cards and taking out loans. The average savings rate in the USA is incredibly low, and achieving financial independence is not possible for most people.

While this may seem rather discouraging, and the global economic state may indicate otherwise, we are actually living during the wealthiest period since the dawn of human existence. In other words, there are many ways and tools present today that can help you enhance your wealth more than ever before. You are more likely to achieve financial independence today than you would be on any other timeline. That said, doing so requires a lot of work and persistence.

What Is Financial Self-Discipline?

Self-discipline, in general, is the act of creating personal boundaries that correspond to your values. Your ability to practice self-discipline is what determines whether you are strong-willed or determined enough to respect the boundaries you set every day, regardless of the circumstances.

To practice financial discipline, you must have clear and specific short-term, mid-term, and long-term monetary goals. These goals should include your spending and saving objectives for the different timeframes you set. When setting these goals, you should also decide how you will measure them. Measuring your progress will help you find out if you're on the right track. Establishing financial discipline is the first step on the ladder to attaining financial freedom.

Unfortunately, things don't always go as planned. Emergencies and unexpected situations happen all the time. We often get distracted, lose sight of our goals, and end up struggling to pick up where we left off. There will always be something that attempts to knock us off track, whether it's an event, a person, a temptation, or a short-term need. However, with self-discipline, we can keep going regardless of all of these inconveniences. Mastering this skill will help you to establish good financial habits that you can sustain in the long run. Only then will you be able to maintain a positive monetary lifestyle. This doesn't necessarily mean that you have to be frugal; it just means you are able to spend your money wisely and ensure that you're secure in case of inconvenience. The goal here is to maintain a balance between living a comfortable and fun life within your financial means.

When you think of financial discipline as a lifestyle, you will eventually achieve financial independence. Being financially independent refers to a person's ability to cover their living expenses without depending on anyone, even if it's their current employer or a credit card. It gives you the flexibility you need to be able to make decisions that serve your short-, mid-, and long-term needs rather than be bound by your current financial status. Financial independence means you can be goal-driven instead of being controlled by your finances.

It sounds too good to be true, right? Well, not necessarily. Understanding the root of your financial problems and the reasons you're struggling to maintain financial discipline is the key to creating discipline with money.

How to Deal with Financial Issues

Everyone knows how stressful dealing with financial problems can get. Unfortunately, many people allow themselves to be overtaken by this type of worry. Getting stuck in your head does not solve anything and can even make things worse. The amount of valuable time and worry you put into overthinking your problems can be directed toward finding workable solutions instead. You can change your unwanted reality and improve your financial situation only by putting together a realistic financial plan that can steer you toward the right path.

It can be much easier to run away from your problems and pretend they don't exist. You can tell yourself that you'll just stop spending money and live off bread and milk alone (horrible survival food choices, if you ask me!) all you want. However, at the end of the day, you know that that's not realistic. As dreadful as it can be, you need to come face-to-face with your current financial situation. Acknowledge your problems and confront all the ways that they're negatively impacting your life. Visualize how stable your life would get, at least gradually, once you start fixing this problem. This way, you can get yourself to commit to your first goal: practicing financial discipline.

Why Do Financial Problems Arise?

Surprisingly, the main reason adults face most financial problems is not that they're not earning enough money. While incomes may be low, the main reason is a lack of self-discipline. This comes from the inability to tell ourselves, "I don't need this now. It can wait until next month," or "I know that I can afford it at the moment, but I'd be better off paying this money on something that's more important." This character issue starts developing in one's early childhood.

Conditioned Response

Think back to your childhood. What was the first thing you did when someone gave you money? Chances are that you immediately thought of all the candy you can buy. Everyone loves candy. It's sweet, but most importantly, it's gratifying! It satisfies your sweet tooth and signals that you did something right whenever someone gives it to you as a reward.

Growing up, you developed what is known as a conditioned response to money. Whenever you receive it, whether it's in the form of a monthly paycheck or a gift, you immediately feel the need to spend it on gratification. You now take income as a sign that you need to do something that instantly makes you happy. Just as your first response used to be, "yay! I can buy yummy sweets now," you ask yourself, "what is something I can spend money on to make me happy right now?"

Do you know why resorts, hotels, and touristic areas sell pretty much useless items like artwork, trinkets, and weird-looking jewelry or purses that no one would ever consider buying in their hometown? Do you know why people spend time bargaining and buying these items knowing that they've paid a lot more than the real value of their purchases and still walk away with the biggest smile? Any financially responsible individual would know not to spend money on this knick-knack. However, marketers and sellers know that we all have conditioned responses that they can successfully capitalize on.

Have you ever gone back home from vacation and asked yourself what you possibly thought when you bought this junk? Well, the answer is simple. When you're on vacation, you feel happy and joyful. Remember how we were all conditioned to associate these positive emotions with spending money? This is why being on vacation creates the subconscious urge to spend your money on anything.

If you think about it, this type of conditioned response plays a huge role in our daily lives. Let's say you wake up and decide to make a quick stop at the mall after work. You tell yourself, "I'm not going to buy anything. I'll just return the shirt and go straight home. "You hit a new milestone at work and then go to the mall as planned. You make the return and then run into an old friend that you haven't seen in a while. Today is a very good day, you tell yourself. Just as you were making your way out, the accessories stand at your left suddenly looked so appealing. You buy that ring that you've always wanted to buy and decide to head back to the car. This is when thought chimes in: "might as well reward me with a cup of coffee," and the cycle goes on.

Reprogram Your Mind with Self-Discipline

Self-discipline is the only way to rewire your mind and break this cycle. You need to fine-tune this character weakness, so you can stop associating the idea of spending money with happiness. To effectively rewire your brain, you need to replace an unwanted belief or thought with a positive yet convincing one. This means telling yourself over and over again that "spending money is bad" is not going to work. While you may know, for a fact, that this habit is detrimental, your subconscious still believes that it's good because it brings you instant gratification.

What you need to do instead is gradually convince yourself that true happiness comes from sustaining healthy financial habits like investing and saving, creating a new conditioned response. You need to be completely certain that saving and investing will serve you a lot more than spending all your money. You may know the facts, but for this to work, you need to involve your subconscious mind. Visualize all the changes that would take place in your life when you start adopting healthy monetary habits. Will you be able to work fewer hours a week? Will you find peace of mind? Would you still have to worry about covering your necessities each month? Imagine yourself in 10 years. Are you still living paycheck-to-paycheck? Think about where you want to be a decade from now. Will your current financial habits get you where you want to be? What do you need to do, and which monetary changes do you need to make in order to get there?

Opening a bank account that you can refer to as "the account to financial freedom" can help get you started. Dedicate this account to long-term deposits. Remind yourself that whatever goes in is not to be spent on anything. This money is there to help you become financially free.

How to Link Happiness with Financial Discipline

Establishing a mental link between happiness and financial discipline is much easier than you think.

This association already starts forming the moment you set financial goals for yourself. We'll feel a sense of accomplishment whenever we do anything that brings us closer to our goals, which will make us feel happy, and in this way, we'll start re-aligning our minds. We feel bad whenever we fall off track or experience setbacks, which makes us want to work harder to reach our goals. Everything you do, especially in the beginning, even if it's as small as depositing your first $10 into "the account to financial freedom," can bring about a sense of accomplishment. It can make you feel like you're finally taking control of your life. The deposited money, in that sense, is no longer just an exchange tool. It starts to hold emotional value.

If you have left-over money at the end of the month, deposit it into the account and watch yourself get excited. You'll feel like you've over-achieved, which can cause you to subconsciously spend less each month. You may be happily surprised to find that you are saving more than you anticipated. Your money will also grow with the added interest. This will encourage you to keep up your efforts.

Why Is It Challenging to Be Financially Disciplined?

The conditioned response that associates spending money with happiness is the primary reason behind one's inability to be financially disciplined. However, other factors make monetary discipline challenging. We are not always conscious of why we go above and beyond our budget, even when we constantly remind ourselves of all the reasons why we shouldn't do that.

Growing up, we mainly learn by observation. You may fold your laundry in a certain way or wash the dishes in a specific sequence just because that's the way you watched your parents do these tasks. Even though these techniques and sequences have no logical reasons behind them, you grew up to do the same just because that's what your parents modeled for you. Similarly, we don't do the things that were never modeled for us in our childhood. If financial discipline wasn't something that your parent's practiced, then it only makes sense that you'd struggle to incorporate it into your daily life.

While some people are naturally wiser with money or are generally more disciplined than others, self-discipline is a behavior that you can learn. If your parents never cared to save money and were in the habit of spending it all as soon as they earned it, you wouldn't know how to put positive financial habits into action.

The fact that the world today offers limitless opportunities and options also makes it incredibly challenging to be disciplined with money. It takes a very strong-willed individual to say "no" to something that they really want, right? The thing about today's markets is that they no longer rely on satisfying our needs. Instead, they have become in control of our needs. Marketers are incredibly skilled at convincing us that we need something, even though we may have never considered wanting it otherwise.

Another reason you may be struggling to be financially disciplined is that you want to buy the things you never had when you were little. If your parents couldn't afford to buy things that made you happy, you may spend all your money on things that bring you joy now. If you have never gone on vacations or gone to nice places with your family, you may try to take your own family on these experiences. You don't want to feel deprived, even if you find yourself in debt.

How to Be Self-Disciplined with Money

1. Learn about Financial- and Self-Discipline

Think of financial discipline as a new skill. Say you study medicine but wish to become a freelance digital marketer. Would you sign up on a freelancing platform and start reaching out to clients and submitting proposals even though you still know nothing about digital marketing? Unlikely. You'd probably enroll in online courses, attend masterclasses, get some on-the-job training, and spend months preparing before taking on your first real project. Learning this skill requires a lot of time, effort, and dedication, and so does becoming financially disciplined.

You need to start by learning what it means to be self-disciplined. Read self-help books, watch helpful videos, listen to podcasts, and try to apply this knowledge to every aspect of your life. You can't be self-disciplined with money but inconsistent with everything else. Be disciplined in your education, exercise, interactions, etc. When you make self-discipline a habit, and eventually your nature, financial discipline will come quite easily to you.

2. Get Inspired

Whether you realize it or not, our subconscious minds are constantly affected by the content we consume. It's good to have fun and binge-watch Netflix or scroll through Instagram from time to time. However, if you want to change something about yourself, whether it's your diet and fitness habits or wish to learn a new skill, you need to make sure that a good portion of the posts you see, videos you watch, or articles you see motivate toward that cause. In our case, you need to seek out content that will inspire you to stay consistent with your monetary goals. Start following financial entrepreneurs and investment accounts, reading books about budgeting (you've already got a head start on that!), and watching educational financial videos. Becoming financially disciplined and working toward financial independence is not an easy feat. However, consuming content that can help you stay motivated goes a long way. Being inspired further fuels your desire to become better with money. Always remember that you're not the first person to walk down this path. So many people did it before you and successfully attained financial independence.

3. Create Helpful Boundaries

Everyone knows that boundaries are the foundation of discipline. You need to be clear about your expectations and the rules that you need to set for yourself and others, so you can get where you want to be. These boundaries are what will help you deal with money and determine the decisions you make.

An example of a money boundary would be "not spending money on food during the week." Keeping within this boundary would require you to buy your weekly groceries during the weekend and cook all your meals at home. Cooking and eating at home instead of ordering take-out or going out to eat during the week can help you save money to spend on things that you like more. Make sure to set good boundaries and, more importantly, feel good, so you can stick to them. For instance, if you're used to going out to eat with your mom every Tuesday, then this rule wouldn't work for you. Forcing it into your life can cause you to drift away from your mom, which would make you feel bad. Think carefully about the financial boundaries you wish to set for yourself, and ensure they're sustainable.

4. Set Realistic Goals and Expectations

You can't wake up and decide to be financially disciplined starting today, nor can you introduce five financial rules into your life all of a sudden. The process takes a lot of time and must be done gradually, so you don't feel pressured and overwhelmed. Everything we do in life is guided by how we deal with money. How often we go out with friends, what and where we study, what we eat, how much we work, and our financial status and habits determine our overall living standards. Changing the way you budget your money and how you handle it, in general, will impact several aspects of your life. Drastic changes can be very hard to keep up with. This is why you have to set realistic goals and expectations. Start small, so you don't set yourself up for failure. Small milestones and achievements will keep you motivated along the way.

5. Be Patient and Self-Compassionate

Progress is not always linear. You will undoubtedly experience setbacks along the way. Don't be discouraged when you spend a little more money than anticipated or if you don't meet your monthly savings goals. The most important thing is that you don't give up when you experience situations like these. You will be tested now and then, making you feel like you aren't as in control as you thought. Be compassionate and patient with yourself.

The link between feelings of joy and the act of spending money starts at a very young age. This makes it very hard to create good money habits, such as maintaining financial discipline when we grow older. Realizing that being self-disciplined with your finances is the key to attaining financial independence can encourage you to make better monetary choices. It will also allow you to break this negative habit and replace it with a more constructive one. Before you know it, spending less and saving more will make you happier than you've ever been before.

Chapter 6: Building a Healthy Relationship with Money

When we think of our well-being, the words "healthy diet," "sleep," and "exercise" come to mind. Very few people realize that the way we deal with money and how we feel and think about it can significantly influence our health. What you may not know is that financial wellness is one of the cornerstones of a person's overall well-being. When we have an unhealthy relationship with our finances, we tend to make detrimental monetary decisions that add a great deal of stress to our lives.

We develop our relationships with money during our childhood. At that time, we start shaping the beliefs we have about money, which essentially influence our financial choices. These beliefs are influenced by our experiences, observations, environment, and how our parents deal with money. People who have unhealthy relationships with money generally hold one of three beliefs: money is of low importance, money is the key to happiness, or money determines a person's self-worth.

The goal here is to build a neutral perception of money. Money is undoubtedly a very important survival tool. We can't cover our basic needs without it. Building a healthy relationship with money can help us get rid of debt and ensure our needs are met. If we start putting healthy financial habits into practice, we can start building our wealth. This way, we can start allocating more money toward the things we love and care about.

Signs You Have an Unhealthy Relationship with Money

You Spend More Than You Make

Allowing your emotions to guide your transactions can be problematic and start a troublesome pattern with the thoughts - "it won't hurt to cheer yourself up with that dress you've been eyeing for a while. Those few extra bucks that you spend on coffee each morning instead of making your own won't surely put a dent in your pockets. You don't really need a new laptop, but the payment plan is the offer of a lifetime." You continue making these seemingly harmless choices until you realize that you have spent far more money than you can afford, and this is when the trouble begins.

A 2019 study found that only 31% of Americans have $1000 or more in savings. Earning a small amount of money or having a few dollars in your savings account is not something to be ashamed of. That said, earning just enough money to cover your needs with no safety net to fall back on can be incredibly risky.

You Don't Like to Talk about Money

Being secretive about your finances or refusing to talk about money with your significant other is another sign that you're struggling with an unhealthy relationship with money. This habit leads to many problems, especially if you've gotten to a point where you try not to think about or confront your financial situation. Soon enough, you will lose control over your finances. Discussing financial matters is frowned on in many communities and cultures around the world, which is why it's understandable if you don't feel comfortable sharing this type of information with others. However, you need to learn to stop feeling ashamed when talking about money, especially if you're in need of help and guidance.

You Feel Guilty about Spending Money

Believe it or not, saving up all your money and feeling guilty about spending any of it also indicates a very unhealthy relationship with money. While we've been preaching the importance of saving throughout the previous chapters, balance is needed to ensure your overall well-being. Remind yourself that you need to reward yourself from time to time, which is perfectly acceptable. The whole point of saving money is to make sure that you live a harmonious, happy, and stress-free life. Depriving yourself defies the whole purpose of budgeting and working toward achieving financial independence.

Save a reasonable amount of money, invest with calculated risks, and carefully plan the money you spend on your needs, wants, and the things you care for.

Why Do We Develop Unhealthy Relationships with Money?

Your environment shapes the beliefs that you have about money. If your parents taught you that rich people are greedy, you'd grow up believing that money makes you evil. If your family was less fortunate, then you may have grown up believing that having money is a bad thing. This belief motivates your willingness to take control of your financial situation, further fueling your poor relationship with money. If you grew up in a community that associated a person's worth with the amount of money they had, then you'll likely spend all your money on luxury items even when you can't afford them.

How to Build a Healthy Relationship with Money

Building a healthy relationship with money requires a lot of hard work and comes with plenty of ups and downs. This relationship is like any other. It has its fair share of problems and is never ideal. However, putting in the right amount of effort, dedication, and commitment can help you establish balance and improve your financial situation.

The following are some things you can do to enhance your relationship with money:

Do Something for Yourself Every Month

Money can help us satisfy our needs and fulfill our goals. But we should also use it to do the things that make us happy. You shouldn't feel compelled to spend all your income on something you believe would bring you mild joy. However, you should aim to reward yourself occasionally, or else you'll burn out. Make sure to factor this reward into your budget.

Have a Positive Mindset

You should aim to have a positive mindset about money and everything that generates income. Your job may be tiring, but you should still be grateful that you have a reliable source of income. You may not have enough money, but you should be thankful that you have enough to cover your needs. Thankfulness and positivity are the keys to a healthier relationship with money.

Don't Cry over Spilled Milk

We are all prone to making mistakes. However, what differentiates us is how we choose to deal with our shortcomings. Think of your setbacks as an opportunity to learn. Instead of beating yourself up for saving less money than you had intended to this month, take the time to figure out what went wrong. Go easy on yourself and move on. This is the only way you'll move forward.

Acknowledge Your Shortcomings

Trying to deny your wrongdoings or coming up with excuses for your financial shortcomings can lead to additional problems. Work towards becoming more transparent and honest with yourself whenever you make a mistake with money, as this is essential to being financially stable.

Don't Forget to Take Breaks

While being on top of your finances is prudent, a break is called for sporadically. You can't possibly always be thinking, planning, and obsessing about money. In an effort to fix your relationship with your finances, this obsessive behavior will be counter-productive. Balance is critical when it comes to dealing with money.

Beware of the Outsiders

You have to be mindful of who you spend your time with. If you spend a lot of time with people with messy financial habits, they could influence you to do the same. Hanging out with people who show off their expensive purchases or individuals who buy everything that seems mildly appealing can hinder your progress. You don't need to cut them off, but you have to be extra careful and conscious of your spending habits whenever you're around them.

Ditch the Comparisons

Never fall into the trap of comparing yourself to others. Your neighbor doesn't have a great relationship with money just because they recently bought a new car or flew their entire family around Europe last month. Don't judge a book by its cover. You don't know the details of other people's financial situations. For all you know, your neighbor may have taken out a loan that they'll now need to pay off for the next five years of their life. Comparing your financial status to other people can destroy your relationship with money.

Being financially healthy allows you to interact with money consciously. It helps you align your relationship with your values and enables you to make purposeful transactions. Financially healthy individuals know when and where to spend their money. They have safety nets and emergency funds, low levels of debt, and are able to save their money easily.

Conclusion

Managing your finances and knowing how to budget your income is a skill you'll need to use throughout your entire life. You can only succeed, live comfortably, and achieve all your goals if you have the necessary financial literacy.

While learning how to budget will ensure that you never find yourself short of money, it will also help you grow in other aspects of your life. It teaches you how to make informed and balanced decisions, set good intentions, prepare for the unknown, and practice self-discipline. Most importantly, budgeting teaches you about financial boundaries. To begin with, you have to be aware of the exact amount of money you can and can't spend, how much money you need to pay off your debt, and how to stay out of debt.

Once you set out on this eye-opening journey, you'll come to realize that you can live off less money than you ever thought possible.

The invaluable information in this book teaches young adults the importance of learning how to budget. Now that you have read through our guide, you understand the basics of budgeting, know how to acquire good spending habits, implement saving strategies, and come up with reasonable and achievable financial goals.

References

5 ways to practice good spending habits. (2020, May 6). https://www.hrccu.org/blog/good-spending-habits/

Basic Elements of a Budget. (2019, October 8). https://www.hfpllc.com/basic-elements-of-a-budget/

Brooke, K. (2014, February 10). How to track your income. https://kalynbrooke.com/your-money/how-to-track-your-income/

Habits, B. M. (2021, September 20). How to save money - 8 simple ways to start saving money: https://bettermoneyhabits.bankofamerica.com/en/saving-budgeting/ways-to-save-money

How to stop spending money: 7 tips and tricks to curb your overspending. (n.d.). https://www.mymoneycoach.ca/blog/how-to-stop-spending-money-7-tips.html

Johnston, J. (2015, June 30). How to set financial goals: 6 simple steps. https://www.incharge.org/financial-literacy/budgeting-saving/how-to-set-financial-goals/

More, R. (2017, February 14). 5 steps for tracking your monthly expenses. https://www.nerdwallet.com/article/finance/tracking-monthly-expenses

Pant, P. (n.d.). How to get into the habit of saving more money. https://www.thebalance.com/getting-into-money-saving-habit-4125552

What does budgeting teach you? 5 important lessons. (2020, March 17). https://bethebudget.com/what-does-budgeting-teach-you

Build a healthy relationship with money. (n.d.). Desertfinancial.com. https://www.desertfinancial.com/news-and-knowledge/build-healthy-relationship-with-money

Eliminate financial problems through self-discipline. (2013, March 5). Brian Tracy. https://www.briantracy.com/blog/financial-success/eliminate-financial-problems-through-self-discipline-financial-independence/

How to develop self-discipline with money. (2022, February 24). Inspired Budget. https://inspiredbudget.com/episode/how-to-develop-self-discipline-with-money/

Margarita Tartakovsky, M. S. (2012, December 13). What it means to have a healthy relationship with money. Psych Central. https://psychcentral.com/blog/what-it-means-to-have-a-healthy-relationship-with-money

www.ingramcontent.com/pod-product-compliance
Lightning Source LLC
Chambersburg PA
CBHW070125230526
45472CB00004B/1420